PREFACE

On December 8, 1993, Title VI of the North American Free Trade Agreement Implementation Act (Pub. L. 103-182, 107 Stat. 2057), also known as the Customs Modernization or "Mod" Act, became effective. These provisions amended many sections of the Tariff Act of 1930 and related laws.

Two new concepts that emerge from the Mod Act are "***informed compliance***" and "***shared responsibility***," which are premised on the idea that in order to maximize voluntary compliance with laws and regulations of U.S. Customs and Border Protection, the trade community needs to be clearly and completely informed of its legal obligations. Accordingly, the Mod Act imposes a greater obligation on CBP to provide the public with improved information concerning the trade community's rights and responsibilities under customs regulations and related laws. In addition, both the trade and U.S. Customs and Border Protection share responsibility for carrying out these requirements. For example, under Section 484 of the Tariff Act, as amended (19 U.S.C. 1484), the importer of record is responsible for using reasonable care to enter, classify and determine the value of imported merchandise and to provide any other information necessary to enable U.S. Customs and Border Protection to properly assess duties, collect accurate statistics, and determine whether other applicable legal requirements, if any, have been met. CBP is then responsible for fixing the final classification and value of the merchandise. An importer of record's failure to exercise reasonable care could delay release of the merchandise and, in some cases, could result in the imposition of penalties.

The Office of Regulations and Rulings (ORR) has been given a major role in meeting the informed compliance responsibilities of U.S. Customs and Border Protection. In order to provide information to the public, CBP has issued a series of informed compliance publications, and videos, on new or revised requirements, regulations or procedures, and a variety of classification and valuation issues.

This publication, prepared by the International Trade Compliance Division, ORR, is on the ABC's of Prior Disclosure. "The ABC's of Prior Disclosure" is part of a series of informed compliance publications advising the public of Customs regulations and procedures. We sincerely hope that this material, together with seminars and increased access to rulings of U.S. Customs and Border Protection, will help the trade community to improve voluntary compliance with customs laws and to understand the relevant administrative processes.

The material in this publication is provided for general information purposes only. Because many complicated factors can be involved in customs issues, an importer may wish to obtain a ruling under Regulations of U.S. Customs and Border Protection, 19 C.F.R. Part 177, or to obtain advice from an expert who specializes in customs matters, for example, a licensed customs broker, attorney or consultant.

Comments and suggestions are welcomed and should be addressed to the Assistant Commissioner at the Office of Regulations and Rulings, U.S. Customs and Border Protection, 1300 Pennsylvania Avenue, NW, (Mint Annex), Washington, D.C. 20229.

Michael T. Schmitz,
Assistant Commissioner
Office of Regulations and Rulings

(This page intentionally left blank)

(This page intentionally left blank)

THE "ABC'S" OF PRIOR DISCLOSURE
Pursuant to 19 U.S.C. 1592
(Section 592, Tariff Act of 1930, as amended)

INTRODUCTION

The following information is provided by U.S. Customs and Border Protection to help you understand the "basics" of prior disclosure. Simply put, this provision of law provides reduced penalties to parties who advise U.S. Customs and Border Protection ("CBP") of noncompliance with import laws and regulations, before CBP, or U.S. Immigration and Customs Enforcement ("ICE"), discovers the possible noncompliance and notifies the party of the discovery of the possible noncompliance. In some cases, the penalty may be reduced to zero! Valid prior disclosures can save you time and money, but all parties (including CBP) must be aware of prior disclosure rules, and play by the rules in order to realize the benefits of this provision of law. The official policy of CBP is to encourage the submission of valid prior disclosures!

It is important to remember that this brochure only involves prior disclosures submitted pursuant to 19 U.S.C. 1592.

We've followed up the "who, what, why, where, when and how" segments with a list of **FAQ'S** (frequently asked questions) involving prior disclosure. In addition, for those parties who have decided to submit a prior disclosure, there is a **checklist** following the **FAQ's** which may be helpful in completing the submission of the disclosure. Lastly, we've provided a copy of the **CBP Regulations** (19 CFR 162.74) governing prior disclosure for your information.

WHO MAY SUBMIT A PRIOR DISCLOSURE TO U.S. CUSTOMS AND BORDER PROTECTION?

Answer: **ANY** party involved in the business of importing into the United States. This includes, but is not limited to, importers, accounts, Customs brokers, exporters, shippers, foreign suppliers/ manufacturers, etc.

WHAT IS A PRIOR DISCLOSURE?

Answer: A <u>valid</u> prior disclosure reveals the circumstances of a violation of 19 U.S.C. 1592. This section of law permits U.S. Customs and Border Protection to assess monetary penalties against parties who make material false statements, acts or omissions in connection with their importations. The material false statements, acts or omissions must result from the parties' negligence, gross negligence or fraudulent conduct. Some typical examples of such violations include undervaluation, misdescription of merchandise, overvaluation, antidumping/countervailing duty order evasion, improper country of origin declarations or markings, or improper claims for preference under a free trade agreement or other duty preference program.

This same section of law (19 U.S.C. 1592) also provides for prior disclosure (19 U.S.C. 1592(c)(4)). Parties are not required to make a prior disclosure. They ELECT to submit the disclosure. If a party elects to make a <u>complete</u> disclosure of such a violation, <u>before or without knowledge</u> of a formal Custom investigation of the violation, the party receives reduced penalties. The penalty is zero if the importations involve unliquidated (i.e., open) Customs entries and no fraud is involved. If the entries are liquidated (i.e., closed or finalized) and no fraud is involved, the penalty is the interest on the loss of duties. If a fraudulent violation is disclosed, the penalty is reduced from the normal assessment of the domestic value of the goods to 1 times the duty loss, or if the violation involves no duty loss, the penalty is reduced to 10 per cent of the dutiable value of the merchandise.

Of course, in all cases involving liquidated entries and duty loss violations, you must tender this duty loss to CBP (see **WHEN** below regarding the timing of this tender). CBP will notify you later about the validity of your disclosure.

The specific rules governing the prior disclosure provision are set forth in the Customs Regulations at 19 CFR 162.74. These regulatory provisions are provided below for your information. By following these rules carefully, you can avoid common mistakes if you elect to submit a prior disclosure.

WHY SHOULD I ELECT TO MAKE A PRIOR DISCLOSURE?

Answer: The obvious reason to submit the prior disclosure is the benefit of reduced penalties. In some cases, parties have saved millions of dollars in potential penalties by submitting valid prior disclosures. However, there are other benefits which often accrue to the disclosing party. Conducting periodic self-assessment of your importing activities and availing yourself of this provision of law may permit you to detect and correct errors, as well as ensure future compliance with Customs laws and regulations. Additional time and money savings often materialize in the form of reduced legal expenses and/or the elimination of lengthy CBP penalty proceedings. Of course, the Government benefits as well by eliminating or reducing expenditures of valuable investigative resources and manpower.

WHEN SHOULD I SUBMIT A PRIOR DISCLOSURE TO U.S. CUSTOMS AND BORDER PROTECTION?

Answer: This involves a judgment call which depends on your particular circumstances. As a general rule, if you can identify the specific import transactions which violate 19 USC 1592, and you wish to submit a prior disclosure, you should do so as soon as possible. Certain factors may exist which will influence your decision. Obviously, if CBP already has contacted you regarding the violation, you may decide to forego disclosure (but see FAQ's below concerning the availability in such cases for additional relief!). Another factor which may influence your decision to submit the disclosure could be that you have not yet assembled all the correct information involving the transactions which are in violation of 19 USC 1592. In this case, the CBP regulations allow you to initiate the prior disclosure, while affording you 30 days after you have initiated the disclosure to assemble this information. You can ask for extensions of time past the 30 days to complete the assembly of this information.

CBP officers frequently are asked about the appropriate time to submit duties that are due involving the disclosed violation. CBP regulations spell out that you should submit any duty loss involving liquidated entries covered by your disclosure at the time you submit the disclosure. However, if you are not sure of the duty loss, you may wish to wait until CBP notifies you of its calculation. If you choose this latter option, the regulations (see 19 CFR 162.74 (c) below) provide for payment of the amount stated by CBP within 30 days of CBP notification. We note that the Regulations do provide for limited CBP Headquarters Review of local Customs duty loss calculations, but parties who qualify for this limited review still must deposit the loss determined by the local CBP office to obtain such review.

WHERE DO I SUBMIT A PRIOR DISCLOSURE?

Answer: You may submit a prior disclosure to any CBP officer at the port of entry where the disclosed violation occurred. If violations occurred at a number of ports, you should list all of the concerned ports in the disclosure and, although not required, it is a good idea to submit a copy of the disclosure to CBP officers at each of the concerned ports. By doing this, CBP will be able to consolidate handling the multi-port disclosure at a single port.

HOW DOES U.S. CUSTOMS AND BORDER PROTECTION DECIDE IF THE PRIOR DISCLOSURE I SUBMIT IS VALID?

Answer: The first thing CBP does is make sure that you have disclosed the circumstances of the violation in accordance with the regulations (see 19 CFR 162.74(b) below). An incomplete disclosure of the circumstances of the violation is the most common error associated with prior disclosure, yet is easily avoidable by following the regulation's requirements. Once CBP decides that you have disclosed the circumstances of the violation, the agency then checks to see that no open formal Customs investigation of the disclosed violation exists, and verifies the accuracy of the information you submitted. If no open formal investigation exists, or CBP determines you have no knowledge of an open investigation, CBP will notify you that your disclosure is valid, assuming, of course, that the information you provided is verified as accurate. If, upon a thorough review of the facts relating to the prior disclosure, CBP determines that there was no violation of 19 U.S.C. 1592, it is CBP policy to refund the duties on liquidated entries tendered with the prior disclosure.

FAQ'S (FREQUENTLY ASKED QUESTIONS)

1. Who in CBP decides whether my prior disclosure is valid?

Answer: The Fines, Penalties and Forfeitures Officer responsible for the port of entry where the admitted violation took place will decide whether the prior disclosure is valid (see 19 CFR 162.74(a)(2)).

2. I've never been contacted by a Customs officer regarding the violation I wish to disclose. Does that mean I qualify for prior disclosure benefits if I fully disclose the circumstances of the violation and tender any duty loss associated with the violation?

Answer: Ordinarily in such cases where there has been no Customs contact, you will receive prior disclosure benefits - but you should realize that CBP or ICE may have commenced a formal investigation of what you wish to disclose before you have submitted the disclosure. In all cases, before submitting the disclosure, you should review 19 CFR 162.74 to assure yourself that none of the events listed there has taken place. These events can give rise to a presumption that you had knowledge of the commencement of a formal Customs investigation. The law is rather specific here. The disclosing party has the burden of demonstrating lack of knowledge of a commenced formal investigation!

3. I have reviewed my import transactions and have discovered a mistake on my entry documents relating to the value of the merchandise. Although the value I reported was too low, I haven't been contacted by CBP or ICE and know that this was not an intentional error. Should I submit a prior disclosure?

Answer: Probably so. You have to decide whether your false statement as to the value occurred through negligent, grossly negligent or fraudulent conduct. If you submit the disclosure and U.S. Customs and Border Protection determines that no violation took place, there are no penalty consequences under 19 USC 1592, and therefore, no record of the disclosure is made. On the other hand, if you submit the disclosure and CBP determines that a 19 USC 1592 violation did occur, you will be granted disclosure treatment for that violation, assuming of course that you fully disclosed the circumstances before or without knowledge of the commencement of a formal investigation of what was disclosed, and tendered any loss of duties on liquidated entries.

4. How do I fully disclose the circumstances of a violation?

Answer: Just follow the requirements set forth below in 19 CFR 162.74(b). These four rather straightforward requirements involve the specifics of the import transactions involved (e.g., merchandise, violation details, Customs entries involved, etc.) and the correct information which should have been provided to CBP.

5. I've discovered certain undeclared importation costs which CBP may consider dutiable. Do the prior disclosure rules permit me to obtain a Customs decision or review on the dutiability issue before I submit the disclosure or tender any duties which might be due?

Answer: First, it's important to remember that the importer is responsible for the truth and accuracy of the information submitted to CBP, including all dutiable elements of the transaction. If you have determined that required costs have not been reported to CBP, we recommend that you consider submitting the prior disclosure. You will be notified by CBP whether any duty tender you submitted was insufficient, and given an opportunity to increase your tender to the amount requested by CBP. In cases where CBP determines the duty loss exceeds $100,000, you may be eligible for CBP Headquarters review of the duty calculation prior to the decision on the validity of the disclosure, but such appeals require the deposit of the disputed amount, are limited in scope, and the Headquarters decision is final. In all other cases, if CBP denies the validity of the disclosure because you failed to tender the correct loss of duties (i.e., failed to acknowledge the dutiability of certain costs), you will be able to challenge such determinations if a subsequent penalty proceeding occurs.

6. Must I submit my disclosure in writing?

Answer: No, but it certainly is recommended that you do so. By submitting the disclosure in writing, you avoid some obvious problems. The scope and details of the disclosure are on paper and the credibility of conversations does not become an issue. Also, although you may make an oral disclosure, it must be followed up in writing within

10 days of your oral communication to a CBP or ICE officer. The problems associated with oral disclosures become glaring in those cases involving hundreds of import transactions, particularly where different types of merchandise are involved!

7. How far back in time should I go in reviewing my transactions and deciding the scope of my prior disclosure?

Answer: This is a very common problem with disclosures. First and foremost, it is essential to remember that you determine the scope of the disclosure. For example, if you make a valid disclosure of 2004 violations and CBP, during its disclosure verification proceedings discovers violations in 2003, you only get disclosure treatment for the 2004 violations. A good rule of thumb to follow in defining the scope of your disclosure is to cover those violations not barred by the statute of limitations, i.e., five years from the date of discovery for fraud, and five years from the date of occurrence for those violations involving gross negligence or negligence violations. It should also be remembered that the scope issue affects CBP as well. For example, if CBP or ICE has an open investigation involving alleged false country of origin covering only your 2004 widget imports, you may be able to obtain disclosure treatment for violations you disclose which occurred before 2004!

8. What is a formal investigation and how does it affect prior disclosure?

Answer: The law provides that when any Customs officer has reason to believe that a possibility of a violation of 19 U.S.C. 1592 has taken place, and the Customs officer records such belief in writing, a formal investigation has commenced (see 19 CFR 162.74(g) below for complete definition). If you submit a clearly labeled prior disclosure and CBP later denies disclosure treatment on the basis that CBP or ICE had commenced a formal investigation of what you disclosed, CBP is required to provide you with notice of the written commencement in a subsequent penalty proceeding. Remember however, that if you can demonstrate that you had no knowledge of the commencement at the time of your disclosure, you may still be afforded disclosure benefits (see 19 CFR 162.74(i) below).

9. I know that CBP or ICE has commenced a formal investigation of my 2004 imports involving undeclared royalties I paid my supplier. May I get disclosure benefits if I disclose merchandise misdescription involving the same shipments?

Answer: Yes, provided the Customs investigation only related to the royalty violations, and you fully disclose the circumstances of the violations involving misdescription (including tendering any loss of duties). Put another way, you may obtain disclosure benefits for additional violations not covered by the scope of Customs investigation.

10. If I submit a valid prior disclosure of a violation of 19 U.S.C. 1592, can I be criminally prosecuted based on the information I disclose?

Answer: If you submit a disclosure containing information which gives CBP reason to believe that a criminal violation has occurred, CBP and ICE legally are obligated to refer that information to the appropriate U.S. Attorney's office. The U.S. Attorney's office then is responsible for making a decision whether to prosecute the alleged criminal violation. Generally speaking, in CBP experience, a validly disclosed, non-fraudulent violation rarely is prosecuted. It should be reiterated however, that the U.S. Attorney's Office makes the decision on prosecution.

11. I have been notified that the Office of Regulatory Audit will be conducting a focused assessment of my 2004 widget importations in 2 months. What should I do before the team arrives?

Answer: It is recommended that you utilize this 2 month period to conduct a self-assessment of your importations. By doing so, if you discover potential violations of 19 U.S.C. 1592, you may obtain prior disclosure benefits if you fully disclose the circumstances of the violations before the audit team arrives.

12. Doesn't the fact that CBP or ICE may commence a formal investigation of a potential violation, and possibly preclude prior disclosure, chill or inhibit a free and frank exchange of information between importers and Customs officials?

Answer: There is no simple answer to this question. On the one hand, CBP and ICE are law enforcement agencies and are required to follow the law when they have reason to believe that a violation has occurred. On the other hand, CBP encourages facilitation of lawful international commerce. Striking a balance between these objectives requires both CBP and the trade to exercise shared responsibilities (one of the principal tenets of the Customs Modernization Act). For example, an importer is responsible for using reasonable care with respect to its importations.

If you're an importer and have used reasonable care with regard to your imports, you shouldn't feel constrained to discuss your importations with CBP. The importer who uses reasonable care is not culpable, and therefore does not violate 19 U.S.C. 1592. Such is often the case where, for example, a CBP import specialist, inspector or auditor merely asks you details about your merchandise. The questions alone do not constitute a commenced investigation.

However, if the auditor, import specialist, or inspector has reason to believe you may have committed a violation, creates a writing memorializing this concern, and asks you specific questions regarding the suspected violation, a formal investigation may be deemed to have commenced, and, depending on the questions the Customs officer has asked you, you may be charged with having knowledge that a formal investigation has commenced. If you then try to make a prior disclosure, it may be denied.

Of course, it is also true that if you provide information to the Customs officer which would cause that officer to believe you have committed a violation of 19 U.S.C. 1592 (i.e., that you did not act with reasonable care) the officer may, in fact commence a formal investigation, and your subsequent attempt to make a prior disclosure may be denied.

An important point to remember about prior disclosure is that it is rooted in fairness , to both the Government and the trade community. For example, if a party submits a valid prior disclosure, the party receives the significantly reduced penalty benefits the law provides. On the other hand, where there is no prior disclosure and CBP or ICE discovers the violation (and the violator has knowledge of a commenced investigation) disclosure treatment is not afforded the violator. This is another reason why U.S. Customs and Border Protection has adopted a policy which encourages the submission of valid prior disclosures.

13. How am I notified by U.S. Customs and Border Protection that my prior disclosure is valid?

Answer: CBP will notify you by means of a 19 U.S.C. 1592 prepenalty notice and set forth the reduced penalty treatment in its notice. The notice will provide instructions regarding payment of any reduced penalty, and also serves as the CBP record of the disclosed violation.

14. Should I make a prior disclosure of my Customs violations if I know that such violations are under formal Customs investigation?

Answer: Again, this is a judgment call which you must make based on your particular circumstances. Some parties choose to disclose circumstances of the violations in cases where they have knowledge of the commencement of a formal investigation of such violations in order to obtain additional mitigation in subsequent Customs 19 U.S.C. 1592 penalty proceedings. In such cases, by providing the details of the violation to U.S. Customs and Border Protection and by exhibiting extraordinary cooperation, the party may obtain mitigation in the form of significantly reduced penalties, even though they do not qualify for prior disclosure treatment! In some cases, the mitigation may be close to the amount afforded a party who makes a valid prior disclosure. Further details regarding such extraordinary relief may be found in Appendix B to Part 171 of the Customs Regulations.

PRIOR DISCLOSURE CHECKLIST (19 U.S.C. 1592)

The following checklist may prove helpful to you if you have made the decision to submit a prior disclosure to U.S. Customs and Border Protection. Answering all of the questions below may assist you in completing your prior disclosure submission.

1. Is your prior disclosure addressed to the Commissioner of U.S. Customs and Border Protection and does your submission indicate your name, address and telephone number? (Note: Although addressed to the Commissioner, the submission must list all of the concerned ports of entry.)

2. Have you identified the class or kind of merchandise involved in the disclosed violation?

3. Have you identified the importation included in the disclosure by Customs entry number, or by indicating each concerned Customs port of entry and the approximate dates of entry? (Reminder: The disclosing party defines the scope of the prior disclosure.)

4. Have you provided the specific material false statements, omissions or acts involved in the disclosed violation and how and when they occurred?

5. Have you provided the true and accurate information or data which should have been provided in the entry? (NOTE: In this regard, remember to specify that you will provide any unknown information or data within 30 days of your initial disclosure if it is not available at the time of your initial disclosure - you can also ask the concerned Fines, Penalties and Forfeitures Officer for extensions of this 30 day period.)

6. Have you calculated any loss of duty involving liquidated entries covered by the prior disclosure? (NOTE: This amount includes all duties, taxes and user fees.) And, if so, have you prepared a check in the amount of the duty loss made payable to U.S. Customs and Border Protection to submit along with your prior disclosure?

7. Have you identified all of the Customs ports where the disclosed violations occurred? (Remember that the submission must list all the concerned ports of entry.)

8. If you are mailing the prior disclosure, have you considered sending it registered or return receipt requested so that the time of disclosure is the date of mailing? (Reminder: Failure to mail the disclosure in this manner will mean that the time of the disclosure will be considered the date of receipt by U.S. Customs and Border Protection.)

CURRENT CBP REGULATIONS ON PRIOR DISCLOSURE
19 CFR 162.74

162.74 Prior Disclosure

(a) <u>In general</u>. -- (1) A prior disclosure is made if the person concerned discloses the circumstances of a violation (as defined in paragraph (b) of this section) of 19 U.S.C. 1592 or 19 U.S.C. 1593a, either orally or in writing to a Customs officer before, or without knowledge of, the commencement of a formal investigation of that violation, and makes a tender of any actual loss of duties, taxes and fees or actual loss of revenue in accordance with paragraph (c) of this section. A Customs officer who receives such a tender in connection with a prior disclosure shall ensure that the tender is deposited with the concerned local Customs entry officer.

(2) A person shall be accorded the full benefits of prior disclosure treatment if that person provides information orally or in writing to Customs with respect to a violation of 19 U.S.C. 1592 or 19 U.S.C. 1593a if the concerned Fines, Penalties and Forfeitures Officer is satisfied the information was provided before, or without knowledge of, the commencement of a formal investigation, and the information provided includes substantially the information specified in paragraph (b) of this section. In the case of an oral disclosure, the disclosing party shall confirm the oral disclosure by providing a written record of the information conveyed to Customs in the oral disclosure to the concerned Fines, Penalties and Forfeitures Officer within 10 days of the date of the oral disclosure. The concerned Fines Penalties and Forfeiture Officer may, upon request of the disclosing party which establishes a showing of good cause, waive the oral disclosure written confirmation requirement. Failure to provide the written confirmation of the oral disclosure or obtain a waiver of the requirement may result in denial of the oral prior disclosure.

(b) <u>Disclosure of the circumstances of a violation</u>. The term "discloses the circumstances of a violation" means the act of providing to Customs a statement orally or in writing that:

(1) Identifies the class or kind of merchandise involved in the violation;

(2) Identifies the importation or drawback claim included in the disclosure by entry number, drawback claim number, or by indicating each concerned Customs port of entry and the approximate dates of entry or dates of drawback claims;

(3) Specifies the material false statements, omissions or acts including an explanation as to how and when they occurred; and

(4) Sets forth, to the best of the disclosing party's knowledge, the true and accurate information or data that should have been provided in the entry or drawback claim documents, and states that the disclosing party will provide any information or data unknown at the time of disclosure within 30 days of the initial disclosure date. Extensions of the 30-day period may be requested by the disclosing party from the concerned Fines, Penalties and Forfeitures Officer to enable the party to obtain the information or data.

(c) <u>Tender of actual loss of duties, taxes and fees or actual loss of revenue.</u> A person who discloses the circumstances of the violation shall tender any actual loss of duties, taxes and fees or actual loss of revenue. The disclosing party may choose to make the tender either at the time of the claimed prior disclosure, or within 30 days after Customs notifies the person in writing of Customs calculation of the actual loss of duties, taxes and fees or actual loss of revenue. The Fines, Penalties and Forfeitures Officer may extend the 30-day period if there is good cause to do so. The disclosing party may request that the basis for determining Customs asserted actual loss of duties, taxes or fees be reviewed by Headquarters, provided that the actual loss of duties, taxes or fees determined by Customs exceeds $100,000, and is deposited with Customs, more than one year remains under the statute of limitations involving the shipments covered by the claimed disclosure, and the disclosing party has complied with all other prior disclosure regulatory provisions. A grant of review is within the discretion of Customs Headquarters in consultation with the appropriate field office, and such Headquarters review shall be limited to determining issues of correct tariff classification, correct rate of duty, elements of dutiable value, and correct application of any special rules (GSP, CBI, HTS 9802, etc.). The concerned Fines, Penalties and Forfeitures Officer shall forward appropriate review requests to the Chief, Penalties Branch, Customs Headquarters, Office of Regulations and Rulings. After Headquarters renders its decision, the concerned Fines, Penalties and Forfeitures Officer will be notified and the concerned Customs port will recalculate the loss, if necessary, and notify the disclosing party of any actual loss of duties, taxes or fees increases. Any increases must be deposited within 30 days, unless the local Customs office authorizes a longer period. Any reductions of the Customs calculated actual loss of duties, or and fees shall be refunded to the disclosing party. Such Headquarters review decisions are final and not subject to appeal. Further, disclosing parties requesting and obtaining such a review waive their right to contest either administratively or judicially the actual loss of duties, taxes and fees or actual loss of revenue finally calculated by Customs under this procedure. Failure to tender the actual loss of duties, taxes and fees or actual loss of revenue finally calculated by Customs shall result in denial of the prior disclosure.

(d) <u>Effective time and date of prior disclosure</u>. -- (1) If the documents that provide the disclosing information are sent by registered or certified mail, return-receipt requested, and are received by Customs, the disclosure shall be deemed to have been made at the time of mailing.

(2) If the documents are sent by other methods, including in-person delivery, the disclosure shall be deemed to have been made at the time of receipt by Customs. If the documents are delivered in person, the person delivering the documents will, upon request, be furnished a receipt from Customs, stating the time and date of receipt.

(3) The provision of information that is not in writing but that qualifies for prior disclosure treatment pursuant to paragraph (a)(2) of this section shall be deemed to have occurred at the time that Customs was provided with information that substantially complies with the requirements set forth in paragraph (b) of this section.

(e) <u>Addressing and filing prior disclosure</u>. -- (1) A written prior disclosure should be addressed to the Commissioner of Customs, have conspicuously printed on the face of the envelope the words "prior disclosure", and be presented to a Customs officer at the Customs port of entry of the disclosed violation.

(2) In the case of a prior disclosure involving violations at multiple ports of entry, the disclosing party may orally disclose or provide copies of the disclosure to all concerned Fines, Penalties and Forfeitures Officers. In accordance with internal Customs procedures, the officers will then seek consolidation of the disposition and handling of the disclosure. In the event that the claimed multi-port disclosure is made to a Customs officer other than the concerned Fines, Penalties and Forfeitures Officer, the disclosing party must identify all ports involved to enable the concerned Customs officer to refer the disclosure to the concerned Fines, Penalties and Forfeitures Officer for consolidation of the proceedings.

(f) Verification of disclosure. Upon receipt of a prior disclosure, the Customs officer shall notify Customs Office of Investigations of the disclosure. In the event the claimed prior disclosure is made to a Customs officer other than the concerned Fines, Penalties and Forfeitures Officer, it is incumbent upon the Customs officer to provide a copy of the disclosure to the concerned Fines Penalties and Forfeitures Officer. The disclosing party may request, in the oral or written prior disclosure, that the concerned Fines, Penalties and Forfeitures Officer request that the Office of Investigations withhold the initiation of disclosure verification proceedings until after the party has provided the information or data within the time limits specified in paragraph (b)(4) of this section. It is within the discretion of the concerned Fines, Penalties and Forfeitures Officer to grant or deny such requests.

(g) Commencement of a formal investigation. A formal investigation of a violation is considered to be commenced with regard to the disclosing party on the date recorded in writing by the Customs Service as the date on which facts and circumstances were discovered or information was received that caused the Customs Service to believe that a possibility of a violation existed. In the event that a party affirmatively asserts a prior disclosure (i.e., identified or labeled as a prior disclosure) and is denied prior disclosure treatment on the basis that Customs had commenced a formal investigation of the disclosed violation, and Customs initiates a penalty action against the disclosing party involving the disclosed violation, a copy of a "writing" evidencing the commencement of a formal investigation of the disclosed violation shall be attached to any required prepenalty notice issued to the disclosing party pursuant to 19 U.S.C. 1592 or 19 U.S.C. 1593a.

(h) Scope of the disclosure and expansion of a formal investigation. A formal investigation is deemed to have commenced as to additional violations not included or specified by the disclosing party in the party's original prior disclosure on the date recorded in writing by the Customs Service as the date on which facts and circumstances were discovered or information was received that caused the Customs Service to believe that a possibility of such additional violations existed. Additional violations not disclosed or covered within the scope of the party's prior disclosure that are discovered by Customs as a result of an investigation and/or verification of the prior disclosure shall not be entitled to treatment under the prior disclosure provisions.

(i) Knowledge of the commencement of a formal investigation. -- (1) A disclosing party who claims lack of knowledge of the commencement of a formal investigation has the burden to prove that lack of knowledge. A person shall be presumed to have had knowledge of the commencement of a formal investigation of a violation if before the claimed prior disclosure of the violation a formal investigation has been commenced and:

(i) Customs, having reasonable cause to believe that there has been a violation of 19 U.S.C. 1592 or 19 U.S.C. 1593a, so informed the person of the type of or circumstances of the disclosed violation; or

(ii) A Customs Special Agent, having properly identified himself or herself and the nature of his or her inquiry, had, either orally or in writing, made an inquiry of the person concerning the type of or circumstances of the disclosed violation; or

(iii) A Customs Special Agent, having properly identified himself or herself and the nature of his or her inquiry, requested specific books and/or records of the person relating to the disclosed violation; or

(iv) Customs issues a prepenalty or penalty notice to the disclosing party pursuant to 19 U.S.C. 1592 or 19 U.S.C. 1593a relating to the type of or circumstances of the disclosed violation; or

(v) The merchandise that is the subject of the disclosure was seized; or

(vi) In the case of violations involving merchandise accompanying persons entering the United States or commercial merchandise inspected in connection with entry, the person has received oral or written notification of Customs finding of a violation.

(2) The presumption of knowledge may be rebutted by evidence that, notwithstanding the foregoing notice, inquiry or request, the person did not have knowledge that an investigation had commenced with respect to the disclosed information.

ADDITIONAL INFORMATION

The Internet

The home page of U.S. Customs and Border Protection on the Internet's World Wide Web, provides the trade community with current, relevant information regarding CBP operations and items of special interest. The site posts information -- which includes proposed regulations, news releases, publications and notices, etc. -- that can be searched, read on-line, printed or downloaded to your personal computer. The web site was established as a trade-friendly mechanism to assist the importing and exporting community. The web site also links to the home pages of many other agencies whose importing or exporting regulations that U.S. Customs and Border Protection helps to enforce. The web site also contains a wealth of information of interest to a broader public than the trade community. For instance, on June 20, 2001, CBP launched the "Know Before You Go" publication and traveler awareness campaign designed to help educate international travelers.

The web address of U.S. Customs and Border Protection is http://www.cbp.gov

Customs Regulations

The current edition of *Customs Regulations of the United States* is a loose-leaf, subscription publication available from the Superintendent of Documents, U.S. Government Printing Office, Washington, DC 20402; telephone (202) 512-1800. A bound, 2003 edition of Title 19, *Code of Federal Regulations*, which incorporates all changes to the Regulations as of April 1, 2003, is also available for sale from the same address. All proposed and final regulations are published in the *Federal Register*, which is published daily by the Office of the Federal Register, National Archives and Records Administration, and distributed by the Superintendent of Documents. Information about on-line access to the *Federal Register* may be obtained by calling (202) 512-1530 between 7 a.m. and 5 p.m. Eastern time. These notices are also published in the weekly *Customs Bulletin* described below.

Customs Bulletin

The *Customs Bulletin and Decisions ("Customs Bulletin")* is a weekly publication that contains decisions, rulings, regulatory proposals, notices and other information of interest to the trade community. It also contains decisions issued by the U.S. Court of International Trade, as well as customs-related decisions of the U.S. Court of Appeals for the Federal Circuit. Each year, the Government Printing Office publishes bound volumes of the *Customs Bulletin*. Subscriptions may be purchased from the Superintendent of Documents at the address and phone number listed above.

Importing Into the United States

This publication provides an overview of the importing process and contains general information about import requirements. The February 2002 edition of *Importing Into the United States* contains much new and revised material brought about pursuant to the Customs Modernization Act ("Mod Act"). The Mod Act has fundamentally altered the relationship between importers and U.S. Customs and Border Protection by shifting to the importer the legal responsibility for declaring the value, classification, and rate of duty applicable to entered merchandise.

The February 2002 edition contains a section entitled "Informed Compliance." A key component of informed compliance is the shared responsibility between U.S. Customs and Border Protection and the import community, wherein CBP communicates its requirements to the importer, and the importer, in turn, uses reasonable care to assure that CBP is provided accurate and timely data pertaining to his or her importation.

Single copies may be obtained from local offices of U.S. Customs and Border Protection, or from the Office of Public Affairs, U.S. Customs and Border Protection, 1300 Pennsylvania Avenue NW, Washington, DC 20229. An on-line version is available at the CBP web site. *Importing Into the United States* is also available for sale, in single copies or bulk orders, from the Superintendent of Documents by calling (202) 512-1800, or by mail from the Superintendent of Documents, Government Printing Office, P.O. Box 371954, Pittsburgh, PA 15250-7054.

Informed Compliance Publications

U.S. Customs and Border Protection has prepared a number of Informed Compliance publications in the "*What Every Member of the Trade Community Should Know About:...*" series. Check the Internet web site http://www.cbp.gov for current publications.

Value Publications

Customs Valuation under the Trade Agreements Act of 1979 is a 96-page book containing a detailed narrative description of the customs valuation system, the customs valuation title of the Trade Agreements Act (§402 of the Tariff Act of 1930, as amended by the Trade Agreements Act of 1979 (19 U.S.C. §1401a)), the Statement of Administrative Action which was sent to the U.S. Congress in conjunction with the TAA, regulations (19 C.F.R. §§152.000-152.108) implementing the valuation system (a few sections of the regulations have been amended subsequent to the publication of the book) and questions and answers concerning the valuation system. A copy may be obtained from U.S. Customs and Border Protection, Office of Regulations and Rulings, Value Branch, 1300 Pennsylvania Avenue, NW, (Mint Annex), Washington, D.C. 20229.

Customs Valuation Encyclopedia (with updates) is comprised of relevant statutory provisions, CBP Regulations implementing the statute, portions of the Customs Valuation Code, judicial precedent, and administrative rulings involving application of valuation law. A copy may be purchased for a nominal charge from the Superintendent of Documents, Government Printing Office, P.O. Box 371954, Pittsburgh, PA 15250-7054. This publication is also available on the Internet web site of U.S. Customs and Border Protection.

Additional information may also be obtained from U.S. Customs and Border Protection ports of entry. Please consult your telephone directory for an office near you. The listing will be found under U.S. Government, Department of Homeland Security.

"Your Comments are Important"

The Small Business and Regulatory Enforcement Ombudsman and 10 regional Fairness Boards were established to receive comments from small businesses about Federal agency enforcement activities and rate each agency's responsiveness to small business. If you wish to comment on the enforcement actions of U.S. Customs and Border Protection, call 1-888-REG-FAIR (1-888-734-3247).

www.ingramcontent.com/pod-product-compliance
Lightning Source LLC
Chambersburg PA
CBHW081433310526
45790CB00020B/3741

9 781508 804857